CW00860051

PUPPY
BEHAVIOUR
THE HAVERS WAY

STEVEN HAVERS

Lulu Publishing Services rev. date: 11/24/2015

Steven Havers' guide to
Your New Puppy.
From a very different perspective.

CONTENTS

FOREWORD

By Matthew Hoggard MBE

As a professional cricketer one of the things that you learn once you've been around the game at the highest level for a few years is that you can never stop learning about the game as it changes and evolves.

With the arrival of 20/20 cricket and the innovations it alone has spawned the game has changed so much since I first began my journey into and around the first class game some 20 years ago.

That ability to adapt and never be complacent or have a fixed 'painting by numbers' approach to any situation is one that I've come to value and look for when I need help with a problem – such as Billy our much-loved but somewhat unpredictable Doberman. Like many dog-owners before us who were planning a family Billy had us between the proverbial 'rock and a hard place'. One evening at the meal table he'd tried to jump on to my lap and when I pushed him away he snapped at me – and he meant it!

Not surprisingly Sarah and I were very upset – not just because he snapped - but also because with the hoped for new offspring not far away a jealous and unreliable Billy was not an option – but then neither was parting with him either.

An Internet search threw up a number of dog training options and we fired off enquiries to several of them. First to reply was Steven Havers – and the fact that we were in Yorkshire and he was in Leicestershire was no problem and neither as we discovered was Billy. To say they didn't get off to a good start was an understatement - but the way Steven dealt with the situation had me impressed from the minute I opened the door to him on his arrival. The trouble was - Billy wouldn't let him in! Unruffled Steven remained on the doorstep talking to Sarah and myself and completely ignoring Billy – for 40 minutes! Eventually when Billy realised he wasn't going to get a response he stopped and Steven was able to step inside.

What impressed me was that he was ready to tackle whatever came his was way because he didn't have a 'script'. From the minute Billy kicked off in the doorway Steven was assessing his behaviour, and ours and was watching and learning about how the three of us interacted and the environment in which we lived with the dog. Only after doing this did he begin to work with Billy and us to put things right and when we began that work the drills and techniques we learned were simple and straightforward.

Steven's not just a dog trainer he's the *complete dog/owner relationship/behaviourist package* and he's also now one of my best mates as – with his no nonsense approach - we hit it off from the minute we first met.

He's very good at what he does – for which me, Sarah, our son Ernie and most of all Billy are very grateful. So if you've got a dog with a problem the solution may just be a few simple steps away. With Steven's help you too can enjoy the 'eurêka' moment we did with Billy when you realise that your dog has been telling you what the problem was – the trouble is you didn't know what to look out for or how to read the signs and signals from him. It really is that simple!

Matthew Hoggard with a German shepherd puppy at a dog show he opened in April 2010.

INTRODUCTION

Dispel the Myths

There are many myths about bringing a puppy into your house and how to begin your life together and this book is going to dispel many of them. This book will help ensure you get off to a much better start.

Now you may not agree these are myths, you may think they are the best thing you can do with your puppy but my experience has proven these interactions make a dramatic difference to your puppy, now and for the rest of his life. The biggest myths are these:

Your puppy needs to play to enjoy being with you,
Your puppy has to meet every dog and
person you see,
Your puppy can be off the lead.

I will explain all of these statements as you get into the rest of the book.

Now I would like to establish a base principle that you also may not agree with:

You will agree that puppies learn very quickly and they learn from us. Whilst that means they can learn all the desirable behaviours we want them to, it also means they will learn the behaviours that are much less desirable just as quickly. In many ways, we are doomed to fail our puppy because of one very important element and that is the way that we think. People, regardless of who we are or where we come from are generally reactive by nature, this usually means we are more likely to tell our puppy off for bad behaviour rather than praise our puppy for being well behaved.

For our puppy, there is no understanding of right and wrong, there is only attention and it is our attention that shapes their behaviour. The more attention we give to behaviour, the more our puppy will repeat that behaviour. Unfortunately for us, we react more to the behaviours we don't want so we inadvertently teach our puppy to misbehave from the outset. The sad thing is this, even though this creates unwanted behaviours, we keep doing it, hoping something will change.

Because of the way dogs think, they are very good at applying a behaviour learned in one environment to every other environment, this means the behaviours they learn as puppies can stay with them throughout their whole life. It is the most accurate example of the expression "reap what you sow"!

Given this, and the myriad of generic information available online and from friends and colleagues, is it any wonder we are unsure at best, at worst totally confused about how to give our puppy the best start in life? That is without even getting onto "socialisation"! That I will leave for a separate book!

This book is going to teach you a different approach that shows you how to start your new life with your puppy from a different and new perspective, that of the puppy. When you appreciate life from their viewpoint, you gain a whole new level of understanding and with the help of these guides, I will help you deepen the bond you have with your puppy and improve the relationship for the whole of your time together. I hope you find the following guide useful.

Steven Havers, Havers Dog Behaviour

Communication
without Speaking

Your puppy does not speak your language and you will never speak your puppy's language so we are left with a problem. We are at a disadvantage, a distinct disadvantage because your dog knows you better than you know your dog.

Why do I say this? Your dog is an expert at communication without speaking and is a master of body language with amazing attention to detail. Your puppy is a very subtle communicator and can communicate with a tilt of the head or a flick of the eye or a twitch of the ear, all of which we easily miss, let alone understand.

Your puppy is amazingly observant and attentive with particular attention being paid to routines and patterns of behaviour. Your puppy then adds to this your speech patterns and from this information is able to accurately predict what you will do and when you will do it, he also learns what you respond to best and he also learns when to interrupt you to get your attention back.

Compare this, and this is a very brief description of the dogs' abilities but compare this to our own abilities. I would hardly call us subtle in our behaviour, we are rarely quiet and we only pay attention to things that interest or stimulate us, we seem to have forgotten that the best way to learn is to watch. This is exactly what scientists do, they learn through observation and controlled interaction and from this they learn to predict patterns of behaviour, in fact they do to the dog what the dog does to us and from their observations they learn about the dog.

I would also like to dispel one more myth that is popular with TVs dog trainers. Your dog knows you are not a dog and does not expect you to try to behave like one. Any training based on this theory will only confuse you and your puppy. Another misconception tries to convince you your dog is trying to dominate you or become top dog but recent research has disproven this theory, even in wolves and wild dogs. Your puppy is not trying to dominate you or be top dog, he is trying to work out what you want from him. Your puppy is completely capable of giving you what you want, he doesn't need bribes or stimulation, he just needs clear communication and calm attention for calm behaviour. Your puppy has worked you out far better than that so for whose benefit do trainers use food? For the simple humans, of course!

To further make my point concerning communication without speaking and the power of your attention, consider this question. Does your puppy learn to misbehave because you give him a treat for being naughty? Does he learn to misbehave because you give him a toy or play with him when he is displaying unwanted behaviour? No he does not because you probably wouldn't give a treat or toy for naughty behaviour because you probably recognise you will be rewarding it but you do use your voice to tell your dog off.

You use your voice even though you know your dog does not comprehend what you are saying because talking is all we know. Your puppy merely comprehends what he is doing generates a great deal of your attention and because your puppy thrives on your attention he will do it more.

Of course, some dogs will stop if you shout loud enough but only because you have scared them or momentarily surprised or interrupted them. This may have stopped your puppy from misbehaving because you have made him scared of you but you have also made your puppy confused and frustrated. I know some owners believe the dog should fear them but that is not the base for a happy and healthy relationship.

The biggest factor working against us is our need to speak. It seems to be such an overwhelming desire; we do seem unable to control it, so much so that we almost seem to have almost no control over our voices in times of doubt or uncertainty. We seem to just speak slower and louder!

I am sure if you are an English person who has been abroad you will have done this when trying to communicate with someone who does not speak your language!

When slower and louder has failed, we then resort to very clumsy and hesitant sign language to accompany our very broken attempts at a foreign language or whilst we are still talking slower and louder. You know how frustrated that makes you feel, dare I say even stupid? Here you are in another country and you can't ask a simple question. I know how that feels and it is not nice. It can be just as frustrating trying to communicate with your puppy, because of the language barrier!

Communication without speaking is very difficult for us to learn and implement because it requires two things most of us are very bad at, practice and patience, yet it will open up a whole new world for you and your dog when you understand and use communication without speaking. But that eludes us because we are completely unaware this is what our puppy needs from us because no one has ever explained it before!

When you learn to save your voice for only rewarding your dog for good behaviour, you will find your dog really enjoys working for you and will quickly learn which behaviours you reward with your voice so he will simply do more of them which generates more verbal praise and so begins a cycle of behaviour that you both want. Cycles of unwanted behaviour are very difficult to break because you keep doing the same thing, so it needs something different to break the pattern doesn't it?

Communication without speaking is a very simple process yet we find it difficult because we are so conditioned to speak, and we continue to speak even though we know our speech and words have no meaning to our dog. We just persist knowing it does not work, desperately hoping it will somehow miraculously change all by itself!

The majority of unwanted dog behaviour is borne out of confusion and frustration. Your dog is confused and frustrated by your constant stream of words yet you expect him to be able to decipher your meaning and what you are asking of him. Clear communication is needed. Save your words and your voice so when you do use them, they genuinely mean something to your puppy because then he will want to listen to what you want.

To sum it up, it is simply show and tell. You need to show your puppy the unwanted behaviour receives no attention at all and then tell him when he is being good and tell him calmly and nicely so he stays calm and nice! It really does work!

Dog Training and Dog Behaviour

What also works against us is traditional dog training because this is based on or is obedience training. This easily becomes the reference we use when trying to teach our puppy how to behave but it is misleading. Obedience training is command or instruction based and teaches your dog to perform specific tasks in association with a specific command. The command usually relates to the dog taking up a specific physical position that is usually marked as correct with either food or a toy. Because this is so specific to a training environment and is completely dependant on you behaving in a very specific way, it really does confuse your dog when you take him out for a walk. Because you use the same commands from your training class but you are outside of that environment so your dog does not have the same associations. This makes it very difficult for your dog to replicate the required actions which in turn makes you rapidly repeat the commands in ever increasing levels of volume and frustration which your dog interprets correctly as confusion, panic and frustration so he gets more and more uncertain about you and your relationship subsequently declines.

Teaching your dog to sit, down, heel etc. or to do tricks can be a good way to interact with your dog but you have to understand you are merely teaching your dog to perform actions to commands, you are not teaching him how to behave.

In your training environment your dog learns to perform tasks to commands for food reward. His association is not transferred to life outside class because everything is different. Some dogs will perform their associated tasks anywhere but this is dependant on you taking your dog into many varied situations and conditions to repeat the training. This can be seen in obedience competitions or talent shows but the dog is merely performing a routine, a routine he has learned. It is unlikely that your dog will know how to be calm for you outside of this routine. Your whole walk can't be an obedience exercise, your dog will want to explore, how do you cope then?

Why are the majority of dogs unable to transfer their performance to the walk? That can't do it because you behave very differently on a walk. You might still take your treats or toy with you on your walk but you don't make your dog walk to heel the whole time you are out. You are more likely to let your dog off the lead to explore, you may get a recall for your food, but if your dog is having too much fun without you then you and your food become worthless. It is then you realise you have no control over your dog because neither you nor your food mean that much to him.

Your confusion and tirade of changing commands convinces your dog he is better off away from you until you have sorted your self out because you clearly do not know what to do. Your dog takes full advantage of the situation and continues to explore. You quite rightly expect your dog to do as he is told, but this does not happen so you continue trying to get the dog back. In doing so, you become more stressed and confused so your dog decides to stay away. It quickly becomes a self-defeating cycle of behaviour.

Your dog behaves the way you have taught him. You may not realise his, but he has learned from your reaction to his behaviour. You will have given him a great deal of freedom in the house to go where he pleases and to do what he pleases, you will have then told him off when he has done something you didn't want. This is typical and very common human behaviour.

He learns how to interact with people by how he interacts with you. If you always greet him excitedly at the front door, he will believe that is how he must greet every visitor to your house and every person he sees out on a walk. If you let him off the lead as a puppy to "socialise" and play with other dogs then that is what he will do and he will still believe he can do that when he is an adult dog. No amount of food will change that belief. He may, if you are lucky pay you a very brief visit for a treat as he continues to race around like a mad thing but you would really like him to choose to be with you because he wanted to, not just because you have bribed him to. The behavioural expectations we set when our dogs are puppies stay with them throughout their lives because we never change our behaviour or our reaction to their behaviour.

Teaching your dog how to behave can be similar to raising children, certainly the communication needs to be different but you can see striking similarities. A spoilt dog does have tantrums if they cannot get your attention, they do get frustrated which can lead to growling, barking and even biting just because they don't get their own way. Time outs do work and removal of privileges is also a powerful tool because these are both consequences for unwanted behaviour, the difficulty is delivering these consequences without giving any attention. If you tell your dog to leave the room, he is getting your attention which defeats the objective doesn't it?

The two biggest factors in our behaviour are our speech and use of eye contact. We usually look at the person we are talking to and we do judge a person by how they use eye contact. Dogs interpret speech and eye contact very differently. Because your puppy soon learns that when you speak to him, you also look at him and give eye contact, speech and eye contact become the two biggest rewards you can give your dog. You may wonder why this is the case? The answer is very simple. When you speak to your dog and give your puppy eye contact, you are giving your puppy your undivided attention. Your puppy has stopped you doing what you were doing and made you give him all of your attention. If a child interrupted you that way, you might consider that interruption rude! But our puppies are allowed to get away with it. When you consider people are always going to give their speech and eye contact when the puppy is being naughty, you can now see why your puppy learns to be disruptive and naughty. When speech and eye contact are applied to the correct behaviour, you will have a well-behaved puppy and later a well-behaved dog. If speech and eye contact are applied for the wrong behaviour, the results can be disastrous!

With dogs, the devil truly is in the detail but once you know what to look for, how to interpret the subtle signs your dog is giving and how to control your own behaviour, you will be able to understand your dog so much better. Then you will be able to have a meaningful conversation with your dog because you will know how and when to interact with your dog, you will learn to see when he asks you a question and how to answer so he understands what you want him to do. It sounds ideal and it does work but remember this:

Having a well-behaved puppy or dog is a way of life because it comes from you, the owner; dog training is about getting a brief performance.

It is important to learn and remember the difference, if you consistently implement the rules of behaviour, you will never need to carry food or toys again. This does depend on you being calm, patient and consistent. If you are not calm, patient and persistent and expect quick results, then feel free to continue down the bribery route as that is the only way you will get what you want. Dogs are not machines so please don't expect them to behave like machines or well drilled soldiers, unless that is your expectation of owning a dog. If it is, I feel sorry for you because you are missing so much, more than you can imagine. Embrace a different approach, challenge yourself to change your own behaviour and watch your dog fly with you.

Puppy Behaviour, The basics

First impressions are everything as your puppy is going to learn all about behaviour from you and the people he now lives with so you would want to make a good first impression, wouldn't you? After all, you have big shoes to fill as you are taking over that most important of roles, that of being his parent. You are now responsible for the upbringing of an animal that may live for a decade or more.

To get off to a very good start, you and your dog deserve a very good education. This is difficult with the amount of books; TV programmes and Internet based information available, let alone all the other dog owners who force their opinion on you! I am going to steer you through the rubbish into a clearer and simpler relationship guide for you and your puppy, whatever the breed!

We make it very easy for our new puppy to learn all about us because from the minute he arrives home, he has attention from everyone, all the time. In the first two days of living with you, your puppy is recognising and learning your patterns of behaviour and which behaviours get the most attention.

4 Top Tips

1. **Start lead training straight away**
2. Keep your puppy calm
3. Don't make your puppy the centre of attention
4. Don't use your hands as toys

Usually you wouldn't dream of putting a collar and lead on your puppy before you even get in to your house but this very different approach to introducing your new puppy to your new house is a very important one, if you want a very well behaved puppy. Change your mindset from "play and excite" to "teach to behave" which will help you think about setting expectations, standards of behaviour and starting as you mean to go on.

If you give your puppy complete freedom when you arrive at home, your puppy will believe that he can do as he pleases. You will also be more inclined to play with him and overexcite him, which leads to most behavioural problems later on. When your puppy is free to roam, he is more likely to make a mistake, which makes you more prone to verbal correction if the puppy does something, wrong. If he is on the lead, you can guide and redirect him onto something he can do and then you can orally praise him so he learns to associate your voice, and therefore reward, with the behaviours you want.

You want to enjoy a walk with your puppy so why not start by walking him around his new house? This also gets your new puppy used to the lead and collar from the start rather than waiting four or five weeks until he can go out for the first time. It means you can teach your puppy to walk with you on a slack lead, for which you will orally praise so you set the example of correct lead walking from the outset. This is so much easier than waiting until your puppy can go outside for the first time because up to that point, your puppy has got used to, and has come to expect complete freedom and will then protest when the collar and lead is attached. His protest is very likely to trigger a reaction in you, which makes his first experience of being on a collar and lead with you a very stressful and confused one. Hardly the right start, is it?

Bad behaviours can nearly always be prevented if we do things differently right from the start. It does require a change of thought process from you because it's not just thinking about what the puppy needs now, it is also thinking about how the puppy will think he should behave as an adult. He will base his adult behaviours on those he learned as a puppy so it is very important to get puppy hood right.

After a few hours when your puppy has explored everywhere on the lead, take it off but do lead work every day so you build on what you have started!

Staying calm and relaxed whilst lead training is essential and just as important is resisting your urge to pull your dog into a heel position. You should never pull on the lead because you are creating a battle that will continue for the rest of your dog's life.

4 Top Tips

1. Start lead training straight away
2. **Keep your puppy calm**
3. Don't make your puppy the centre of attention
4. Don't use your hands as toys

It seems to be considered normal to excite and wind up puppies. We seem to be absolutely convinced we should play with our new puppies until they drop! It is easy to forget this new addition is a baby because he can see, hear, move and make noise and he loves to chase things!

But does he? He is certainly curious and wants to explore his new surroundings; he does like things that move but that does not mean that's all he wants to spend his waking hours doing!

How can you get to know your puppy or him get to know you if he's charging around like a mad dog?

I do appreciate it is difficult to be calm because you and your family are not calm. You have a brand new puppy to play with and everyone is very excited, you may even have taken time off work to spend with your new puppy or you may have arranged his arrival for a weekend when the whole family is at home.

The first two days that your puppy is in his new home are critical as these are when the puppy learns about his new environment and how to behave. Unfortunately, this is when you are giving your puppy the most attention so it is easy to see how expectations are set, if your puppy gets attention all of the time and he gets the attention for being very excited which means he will come to expect attention for being excited all of the time. This is the very beginning of separation anxiety that can be a very damaging behaviour! It is impossible for you to give your puppy all of your attention all of the time. You have to go to work; the children have to go to school, college, university or work depending on their age. Your puppy is then without all the attention, this causes high stress and usually leads to destructive behaviour.

Quiet time spent with your new puppy in the initial stages of settling in is the best investment of your time and will be far more productive in the long run than high-energy activities. If all you do with your puppy is play, your puppy will come to regard you as a toy that he can play with whenever he wants to. Should your puppy be thinking of you as a plaything because this can be quite unpleasant when the dog is fully mature? The last thing you want is a mature dog thinking he can do what ever he wants with you, especially when you are trying to make him behave. Always remember, with dogs you reap what you sow!

I hope, when you were discussing getting a puppy and planning when to get him, your vision of having a dog is one you can take anywhere, he is calm and relaxed on his lead, calm and relaxed around other dogs and comes back when called. These behaviours all find their roots in puppy behaviour are all achieved by teaching your puppy to be calm and relaxed with you from the outset and it works!

I spend a great deal of my time working with families who have young dogs that are getting out of control simply because they have been over excited as puppies, it then takes hard work to redress their expectation. Prevention is always better than cure and the best foundations are strong ones, if the reality of living with your puppy is different from your vision then your puppy is out of balance and you will need help to put this right.

4 Top Tips

1. Start lead training straight away
2. Keep your puppy calm
3. **Don't make your puppy the centre of attention**
4. Don't use your hands as toys

You will probably have heard of and are familiar with the term "Diva"

A **diva** (/ˈdiːvə/; Italian: [ˈdiːva]) is a celebrated female singer; a woman of outstanding talent in the world of opera, and by extension in theatre, cinema and popular music. The meaning of diva is closely related to that of prima donna.*

Diva is a description also associated with celebrities who expect and demand a great deal of attention, usually with extreme requests. Dogs who, from the outset, receive a great deal of attention can easily become Divas as they learn that the more extreme the behaviour, the greater the attention they generate. Simply because people always give more attention to the behaviours we don't want so the dog does more of them.

Dogs that are prepared go to extremes to get attention are by far the most potentially dangerous because they will have learned to bite at a very early age, usually because they have experienced high energy play their owners and have already risen to the level of nipping. Once dogs learn extreme behaviours generate extreme levels of attention and this pattern is allowed to develop and escalate, there is usually one outcome because at some point the dog will cross the line that we deem uncross able, they will bite. The

* Source: Wikipedia http://en.wikipedia.org/wiki/Diva

fact that is always overlooked when a dog bites a person is the levels of behaviour are always preventable but people the dog has lived with always start them. You can only prevent these behaviours if you are well informed and prepared to put the work in.

This is why it is important to have a calm and relaxed puppy rather than one that expects and gets a great deal of attention. Now here the choice is entirely yours and I urge you to choose carefully. After all, it is the rest of the dog's life we are talking about! Make the wrong choice and your dog's life may be cut short simply because of your behaviour! A calm puppy is a happy puppy; your puppy does not need to be playing every waking moment to be having fun that is a very common misconception!

4 Top Tips

1. Start lead training straight away
2. Keep your puppy calm
3. Don't make your puppy the centre of attention
4. **Don't use your hands as toys**

I hope the reasons for this are obvious to you but that may not be the case! Remember the way a dog learns, what is OK as a puppy is still OK as an adult. Now lets think about those teeth! Puppies explore with their teeth so playing with your puppy and overexciting them with your hands actually makes your puppy to bite you. Yes you did read that correctly, you actually make your puppy bite you. That would lead to a question wouldn't it? Why does that make my puppy bite me? When your puppy is over stimulated, uncertain, scared or very confused, he will try and communicate that to you and he will also ask you to stop the very activity that he doesn't like. As with all his subtle requests, we ignore these until your puppy is forced into desperate measures. He is forced to bite you to try and make you stop winding him up. He genuinely doesn't like it you see! OK, you might think it's ok because it might not hurt when the teeth are vey small or you may find it a cute or endearing behaviour! However, you will not find it as cute and it will be much more painful when the dog is a juvenile or an adult.

I will go even further, no part of your body should be considered a toy by your puppy. Your feet are usually the closest part of you to your puppy when you are standing up which means your puppy may want to bite your trousers whilst you walk around. Again, this may be amusing to you when they are small and easy to manage, which will be very different when they are adult, mature and confident! Puppies naturally chase things that move and this is usually triggered by play, we move toys, the puppy is stimulated by movement and chases the toy. However, the puppy does not restrict this to just toys, oh no! He applies it to everything that moves and if the chasing attracts attention that is even better for him so he will do it more.

Playing with your puppy is purely a human requirement; it is not essential or required from your puppy! My advice is again a bit strange but it is this, don't play with your puppy! I have had many German shepherd dogs from puppies and have never played with any of them and as a result I have very calm and well-behaved dogs. If you insist on playing, it needs to be done properly, at a level and duration the puppy can cope with, with ceilings of excitement, consequences of behaviour and rules of engagement, this is dealt with in much more detail later in this book.

A good, healthy relationship is built on trust and mutual respect yet people seem determined to make life as confusing and as stressful for their dog as possible. Behaviours we encourage as puppies suddenly become unwanted just because the dog has grown, yet the dog just thinks he is doing what you want him to do. He hasn't changed, just got bigger and this is why I ask you to think about the future when you are playing with your new puppy.

Ask yourself if what your puppy is doing would be acceptable as an adult and then hopefully you can make the right choice!

Why Use the Lead
Straight Away?

This is unusual advice for puppy owners and if you read on you will understand why...

This was touched on in the previous chapter but it is very important so I want to go into more depth and detail so you get off to the best start by understanding how a lead should work and how to use it properly.

4 Reasons To Put The Lead On

1. Your puppy won't know how to behave.
2. Puppies explore with their mouths.
3. Puppies do not recognise danger.
4. Puppies do not know your house

I won't separate these bullet points with an individual answer as I have in previous chapters as the answers are all related.

All of the points listed above are true yet we rarely consider them. To help you understand these points from a human point of view, come with me on a little journey in our imagination.

Picture yourself in an environment that is completely strange to you. A holiday to a new country that you haven't been to before is a good example. A new place where you don't know the customs and you don't speak the language. You don't know who is friendly or how things work. You don't even know what the currency is or where the shops are. You can't even ask for help to find a public toilet.

What if you arrived at the airport and there was no help or assistance waiting for you? You would stand in the airport looking confused, lost, bewildered and uncertain. How would you then feel if lots of people all came up to you talking loudly in a language you didn't understand, staring at you, touching you and pushing things into your face and hands?

How would you feel? What would you do? Where would you go? Would you be able to relax, take things in and think clearly?

Of course not, you would probably be very scared and uncertain.

However, if you have organised your holiday through a travel agent or travel company, there will be somebody to meet you at the airport who speaks your language, can help you with customs and guide you to your hotel transfer transport. You are able to relax and enjoy your surroundings because of your guide who knows how things work. This takes a great deal of the uncertainty and stress out of the situation doesn't it?

I hope you're getting the picture and understanding the point I'm making because the first example quite accurately describes how your puppy feels upon arriving in your house. There is no one there that speaks the language and nothing makes any sense at all. The people around your puppy are making lots of noise and moving very quickly but not making any sense. Your puppy is trying to interpret its brand-new environment as well as trying to understand you and your family. The people are touching, prodding, picking him up, making him chase things, how would you solve problems in a similar situation? Imagine how grateful you would be if a nice, friendly local befriended you and looked after you. How much better would you feel then?

So, guess what your role is with your new puppy? Exactly, you are the guide, the befriending local who takes on the confused new arrival. It's quite a challenge but you will handle difficult situations very well with it because of the information I am giving you.

Putting your puppy on a lead when it arrives in your house for the first time turns you into the equivalent of a tour guide and mentor. With the lead, you are able to show your puppy your new home one room at a time, calmly and slowly whilst being in control of your puppy's movements. If your puppy has complete freedom and can run freely through your house doing whatever he wants, he won't want to do as you want. He will object when you eventually put his collar and lead on because he has not been used to being restricted. If you also follow him around when he is off the lead and you are talking to him, you are setting behavioural precedent that you follow your dog. This is exactly what you don't want your puppy to believe. When you have the lead on and your puppy goes to explore something that you don't want him to, you can prevent that by holding the lead. You can then click your fingers to attract your puppies' attention; this will encourage your puppy to come to you for your attention, away from the distraction. You can then reward with nice calm praise, this is the start of your recall training! Why wait to start something so important?

This teaches your puppy a very important lesson.

It teaches them that coming back to you gets the attention, not exploring and putting things in their mouth.

It is then your task to ensure consistent replication of this wherever your puppy is going to be allowed to be. For every room and in the garden there needs to be rules and your puppy needs to understand how you want him to behave and you can only achieve this properly by showing him. Make sure you practice the basic recall training in each room and in the garden and then keep doing it in every possible location so your puppy understands your recall whatever is in front of him.

This also achieves another important milestone in setting behavioural standards with your puppy because it also teaches your puppy how to walk on the lead for you. Whilst walking your puppy around your house, praise your puppy whenever he is walking with you on a slack lead. He doesn't have to walk at heel on your left side; he just has to be calm and his lead slack. Give the most of your attention to the behaviour you want but praise calmly and slowly.

So you can now start to see what can be achieved with your new puppy if you start off with a different mindset than the one you were perhaps going to start with.

It is essential to realise the behaviours we allow, as a puppy will become the behaviours that the dog thinks are still allowed when he is full-grown.

It is a fact of life that behaviours we find endearing in puppies are rarely as endearing in an adult dog and this one of the most difficult facts to face as the owner of a new puppy. Your new puppy is there in front of you, all cute and cuddly and every fibre of your being wants to pick him up and cuddle him. You want to play with him and make sure he likes you, of course you do but you are putting your own needs first, you want to pick him up, you want to cuddle him, you want to play with him but have you ever considered what he wants and needs?

When do we ever consider what your new puppy wants? Rarely, if ever because no one has ever asked you to do that! We allow our own desires to overtake us which means we fulfil our own needs and desires at the expense of the puppy.

It is human nature to do this but human nature is not dog nature, not even domesticated dog nature. I know we buy a dog or a puppy for our own reasons, for company, for the family, to look out for us, to look after us and these are all very good reasons but surely the needs of the dog should be considered!

Of course, as you read this you agree the needs of the puppy should be considered but you can only consider the needs of your new puppy if you know what they are! Certainly, in my extensive experience, the owners with whom I work want to know the needs of their dogs, which is why they come to me but there is very little information available so it is no wonder so many owners don't know what their puppy needs. I hope this guide goes a long way in rectifying that and you start to view your puppy from a different perspective.

Your Choice of Puppy

4 Top Tips

1. **Choose a breed you have experience of**
2. Choose the right sex
3. Choose the right temperament
4. Research requirements, health issues if pedigree and costs

In all aspects of life, experience is everything and there is no easy way to get experience. You learn best when you do things for yourself and to make your own mistakes. If you have had dogs before, then you will, hopefully, have learned a great deal about living with dogs. It doesn't mean you are fully prepared for your next one though or you are sufficiently aware of your dogs needs!

What if you have never had a dog of your own and are looking to get a dog for the first time? Having dogs as a child doesn't really count because the care, feeding and walking would be done by your parents and your role was much more play based. So if you have never had a dog, what can you do as well as reading books to find the right breed for you? I would suggest that you talk to as many dog owners as you can to learn about different breeds and breed characteristics but remember these traits only truly apply to the individual who owns the dog, they will not apply to you. Just because you see someone with a very well behaved spaniel, does not mean you will have a well-behaved spaniel. A great deal of work goes into getting a well-behaved dog and you need to be prepared for this. A mere six weeks in a puppy class is nowhere near enough, particularly as the dog changes the most from six months onwards.

It is true, some breeds are more challenging than others but individuals can be different from the breed generic if you choose carefully! It is the character of the dog that matters most, a very confident dog, whatever the breed will be too much for a less confident owner so try to choose a dog that suits your character and capabilities, they will suit you much better in the long term. My top tip for choosing a puppy is to ask the breeder which is the most confident puppy in the litter and which is the least confident. Then choose one of the other puppies as; hopefully this will be a calmer dog and more suited to being a calm family dog. Remember this is only a tip, not a guarantee!

4 Top Tips

1. Choose a breed you have experience of
2. **Choose the right sex**
3. Choose the right temperament
4. Research requirements, health issues if pedigree and costs

The choice of gender is an important consideration because different genders can bring different challenges but again here there are many myths that can confuse you. Up until February 2014 I had four German shepherd dogs, three males and one female and have no real preference but you need to consider what you prefer.

The obvious differences are females have seasons approximately every six months and this obviously affects her behaviour during this time, she is also of higher interest to males but not as much as you may have heard. I didn't get queues of dogs at my house when my female is in season; even my males remain relaxed and calm. If you choose a female and you don't want to breed with her, then sterilisation is an option but let her have two seasons and reach two years of age before you do as she will be better equipped to deal with the huge changes sterilisation will bring, it can take two months for the dog to get used to the hormonal changes and then she will still be a slightly different dog than before so consider carefully before you act. My own female was fully intact at the age of 12 and was in fine health until her death, which resulted from her back legs failing!

Males can be assertive, confident and a challenge. But these traits can also shared by females so it comes back to choosing the right temperament for you. If you can, see both of the parents, as your puppy is a mix of them, what you see is largely what you can expect to get. I will point out here that mixed breeds do tend to be calmer by nature than pedigrees but still choose wisely and carefully. Many vets will try and persuade you to castrate your dog as a preventative measure but recent research suggests castration to resolve behavioural problems can make them worse.

Since my female died, I have four male German shepherd dogs; they are entire and are very well behaved. I wouldn't consider castration unless there was a genuine medical reason for it. Behavioural problems can usually be resolved with professional help provided that help addresses your own behaviour!

When you have decided which gender of puppy you want, don't rush to buy the earliest available and don't be swayed by the breeder because they will try to sell you what they have got. If you want a female and there are only males left, go and find another breeder. You are going to be living with the dog, not the breeder and some breeders won't give you a second thought once your cheque has cleared! It is your money and your choice so take your time and make the right choice for you.

4 Top Tips

1. Choose a breed you have experience of
2. Choose the right sex
3. **Choose the right temperament**
4. Research requirements, health issues if pedigree and costs

Your new puppies temperament and character will either make your life with your dog easy or it will challenge you depending on its confidence levels. Your puppy's temperament is the foundation of the dog and the basis on which your new puppy will make decisions. The first thing to consider is your own temperament because your puppy will learn to behave by watching you! If you are a nervous, reactive and anxious individual, you definitely need a calm and steady dog. If you are a calm, relaxed and patient person, you are better equipped to deal with more excitable and lively dogs. Certainly, you can have a confident and assertive dog but if your character is not so strong, it will be hard work for you with a dog that pushes his luck. If you are too willing to please your dog, your dog is more likely to spot that characteristic in you and take advantage. I hope you can now see that you need to give a great deal of time and consideration when you choose your puppy! There is much more to it than just buying the first puppy you see.

Also consider your lifestyle, preferences and the amount of time you have available. If you are busy and only have time for one walk a day, then a very relaxed dog like a rescue Greyhound would suit as they love to be quiet and relax. If you have more time and you like going for walks then a more energetic breed might suit but remember exercise! Many people get confused about exercise and believe that you must exercise your dog to the point of exhaustion. This is very difficult to do as dogs have incredible stamina and just get fitter! That amount of exercise also takes up a great deal of time, perhaps you don't have the spare time to give your dog huge amounts if exercise. How can you then give your dog the exercise to tire them?

The answer is to make your dog think! Your dog is intelligent and dogs love to solve puzzles. I don't mean teach your dog to do tricks or find food or toys you have hidden because that is very easy for your dog. We forget the dog's primary sense is smell! Putting something out of sight causes us problems, but our dog will just sniff where you have been, then smell the object you last touched and find it! Not that difficult really when you think about it, is it?

The best puzzles are those that really challenge the dog, getting your dog to find out which of his behaviours get the most attention from you really makes him think. When you only give your attention to the calm ones, your dog will give you more calm behaviour provided you give your attention! There is no finer way to make your dog think than to be selective in which behaviours you reward and to be consistent at it.

You need to be able to trust your dog and your dog needs to be able to trust you. You want a dog you can take anywhere and be proud of. The temperament and character of your dog will determine the ease or difficulty you will encounter when teaching him how to behave, it has a direct impact on your developing relationship. Please also be aware of this; just as not all people are compatible, not all dogs are going to be compatible with you so do your research well and look at the puppies parents for a good idea of what your puppy will be like! Be strong and wait until you find the right dog.

4 Top Tips

1. Choose a breed you have experience of
2. Choose the right sex
3. Choose the right temperament
4. **Research requirements, health issues if pedigree and costs**

All breeds of dog have their own quirks and health issues. Get to know the breed you are interested in regarding feeding, bedding and housing and exercise requirements. If you are considering buying a pedigree dog, what health issues affect your chosen breed? Read up on these so you can ask informed questions of breeders as this will help you decide which breeder to buy from. If breeders carry out health checks like hip and elbow scoring, blood, eye and hearing tests, depending on the breed then they should be responsible breeders as they are ensuring they are breeding from healthy animals.

Do not buy off the Internet or from a bloke you met in the pub. Don't meet in a lay by and buy a puppy, it may be cheaper but you will pay more in the long term and you are fuelling puppy farms

Costs can be high for owning a dog. Food, equipment, bedding, insurance, vets bills, training to name a few and these can all add up. To make sure your puppy is going to have a long and happy life with you, you need to make sure you can afford the dog and afford to get help should you meet with any problems later in life with training or behaviour issues. If you go on holiday, you will have to pay for someone to look after your dog, either kennels or boarding. If you take your dog abroad, you will need a pet passport, all of these things add up!

Rescue centres are full of dogs that became too expensive to own, especially if the owners circumstances changed. I know the future is always uncertain so you can do things to reduce the additional costs like feeding raw food and researching the most recent thinking on annual boosters. Feeding raw food has huge health benefits for your dog and choosing to have blood tests to see of your dog needs boosters rather than just doing it also has health benefits. All puppies need their initial vaccinations at 8 and 12 weeks and they also need their first booster, after that you can make an informed choice! Healthy dogs live longer and cost less!

Puppy Collection Day

Top Tips for Collection

1. **Be as relaxed as you can**
2. Your puppy will be stressed, don't match that behaviour
3. Hold your puppy but don't stroke, fuss or speak as that will reinforce stress
4. Sit in the back, have your puppy on your lap and relax. Give your puppy time to adjust to all that is new, don't overload your new puppy
5. Only stroke and talk when your new puppy is calm and relaxed.

You must be joking, keep calm on the day we collect our new puppy?

I know it sounds a strange thing to say and I know it is immensely difficult to remain calm and relaxed when you collect your new puppy but this book is all about starting as you mean to go on. Up to this point you may have been agreeing with me, you can see my methods make sense but this where the work starts. This is where you start to work hard to control your instincts and relax. A lot of preparation and planning that has gone into this day, you may have been visiting to see the puppies but today is the big day. The trip probably has the whole family involved and there will have been arguments over whose knee the puppy will sit on. You have probably planned the journey for a Friday so you can have the whole weekend getting to know your new puppy or worse still, you may even have taken time off work to spend time with your new puppy so it is no wonder it is such a big event in your lives.

However, these very typical emotions of excitement, anticipation and expectation tend to have the opposite effect than those we intend and can set expectations that ultimately we are unable to fulfil. When expectations are set and then not lived up to, your puppy will become stressed and confused by your mixed and conflicting messages. Your puppy just cannot decipher or interpret your messages and communication correctly, correctly, that is, from our point of view. You will soon learn as you read this book that your puppies interpretation of what we do is very different from our perception of what our behaviour means to our puppy.

It comes down to clear and consistent communication but clear and consistent communication that your puppy understands. It also comes down to knowing how to deal with your puppy's behaviours as they occur so your communication to your new puppy remains clear and consistent.

When you base the very start of your relationship with your puppy in this way, you are making the start of a wonderful journey from the best possible position.

Just as you will be excited and happy at collecting your new puppy, your new puppy will be stressed, confused and scared.

His whole world is changing faster than he can understand. He has left his Mum, brothers and sisters and has been thrust into a brand new world where everything is much bigger and louder than he is used to. Imagine living in a small village all your life and then being dropped into the middle of London. You would find that overwhelming and very daunting!

As with all dogs, your puppy has an inbuilt desire to please and from the outset he will be trying to work out what you want him to do. Until you read this book, no one will have told you that the only way he learns is from your reaction to his behaviour. So also remember this please, if you visited your new puppy before he was ready to come home with you, you have already set expectations for his behaviour. If you played with him at the breeder, you set the expectation that this interaction is how you will always interact with him. When you collect him, these are reinforced and further established all the way home so he is working you out even before you take him home.

This is why this guide is so useful because it will make you much more aware of what you are doing and how you create behaviours in your new dog. All dogs benefit from correct interaction, with new puppies you have a blank canvas to work with, make your picture a beautiful one!

Top Tips for Collection

1. Be as relaxed as you can
2. **Your puppy will be stressed, don't match that behaviour**
3. Hold your puppy but don't stroke, fuss or speak as that will reinforce stress
4. Sit in the back, have your puppy on your lap and relax. Give your puppy time to adjust to all that is new, don't overload your new puppy
5. Only stroke and talk when your new puppy is calm and relaxed.

Your journey home is the start of a great adventure for all of you yet it is the first time your new puppy has been alone with you and it will be a very confusing time for you all. It is probably the first time he will have been in a car.

Many puppies develop carsickness or other stress related associations when travelling and these start with their very first journey. It is not surprising that puppies are sick in a car. They are anxious and scared, their new family is pouring attention on them continuously, which merely overloads the stress levels that your puppy can handle. You will see your puppy is stressed and you will be inclined to try to reassure your puppy but you are merely rewarding and reinforcing the stress and anxiety, making it a powerful association when placed in a car. The best thing to do is don't try to reassure your puppy, just let your puppy feel that you are calm and relaxed, keep the car at a cool, comfortable temperature and make sure you all talk calmly.

As the journey progresses, you will notice when he calms down and visibly relaxes, then you can stroke and praise him so he learns to associate calm and relaxed behaviour with your attention. This creates an association and a belief that traveling in a car is calm and relaxed so in the future you will be able to enjoy adventures together traveling to new places and he will be fine in the car. This really opens the world up to you and your new dog so it is important to set the right standard of behaviour from the outset

It is always easier to prevent bad behaviour and associations from starting than it is to cure them, especially with a puppy so take a different view on how you behave when you collect your new puppy.

Top Tips for Collection

1. Be as relaxed as you can
2. Your puppy will be stressed, don't match that behaviour
3. **Hold your puppy but don't stroke, fuss or speak as that will reinforce stress**

4. **Sit in the back, have your puppy on your lap and relax. Give your puppy time to adjust to all that is new, don't overload your new puppy**
5. **Only stroke and talk when your new puppy is calm and relaxed.**

I have combined these three points as they are interrelated. When the puppy is in the car, place the puppy on the seat next to a family member on the backseat. Put your puppy on a blanket, ideally one that smells of his mum so he can relax and settle down. If you avoid excitable petting and fuss, your puppy will settle down and relax before the journey starts. When he does settle, interact with very calm stroking. Don't drive off straight away, start the engine and wait for a couple of minutes so you give your new puppy time to adjust, remember everything is new and is very uncertain.

By doing this, you let your puppy experience the environment of the car in his own time and from a calm perspective. Do not have the temperature too high as the puppy won't be used to it and keep the car cool with windows slightly open to ensure plenty of fresh air. Try to avoid using the air conditioning, as this will dry the air, which your new puppy won't be used to.

Drive your car as carefully and considerately as you would with a new human baby in the car. This will give your puppy a smooth and pleasant experience of traveling with you and this will build a positive experience. Make more stops than you would usually do and take your puppy for a walk around when you do stop. Make sure you carry your puppy and put them down briefly to see if the toilet is needed. This also helps take the stress off the puppy and prevents stress build up, which will help puppy deal with the journey.

Make sure you continue to stay calm and relaxed and only stroke your puppy when he is calm and relaxed.

That is a great deal to remember and a great deal of responsibility. The journey home is one you will need to have considered carefully and prepared for even more seriously. Now please consider this, your puppy will begin to work out your behavioural patterns in the first two days of living with you. Yes, that quickly so your initial time in the car is the best time to make a good first impression!

You see how important it is that the relationship is based on a solid and clear foundation so you both understand what is required from the other and what is not. The differences will define your success or failure to properly communicate with your puppy.

Arriving At Home
With Your Puppy

Getting off to the right start with your new puppy at home.

4 Top Tips on Arriving Home

1. **Try to refrain from explaining your home to your puppy.**
2. Put a collar and lead on your puppy before you go into the house.
3. Take your puppy into each room on his collar and lead.
4. Do not reward excitement; calmly praise your puppy for being calm, thus establishing the correct associations from the word go.

Arriving at home for the very first time is a very exciting experience for you and your family and there will be intense competition to decide who gets to do what with the puppy. This excitement establishes benchmark behaviour for your puppy because your puppy will believe that everybody always behaves in this way at home so your puppy will match your behaviour. In your excitement, you will interact with your puppy when you are both excited. This merely demonstrates to your puppy that this is how you want him to behave always because it is the first thing you have shown him. Remember the importance of creating a good first impression. Everything is happening for the first time so you need to remember to set a good example with your calm and relaxed behaviour and by praising his calm and relaxed behaviour!

Instead, try to make your arrival at home a quiet and relaxed occasion, it is very easy to get too excited and overload your puppy so the quieter and more relaxed you are, the better he will handle the situation and the easier he will find it to give you the behaviour you want!

If you have children, this step will be difficult as they are going to be very excited yet it is even more important that the children behave correctly with the dog whilst he is a puppy to ensure that your puppy knows how to behave with your children when he becomes bigger, stronger, more confident and with bigger teeth! Your children's behaviour should have been discussed and agreed in your planning and preparation before you got your puppy and they will have to work hard to contain themselves. Encourage and praise them for being calm and relaxed around your puppy so your children and your puppy all learn to be calm and relaxed together! That's what you want, isn't it?

Children should never treat dogs as toys and dogs should not treat children as toys as this is rarely going to turn out well. Set limits of behaviour for your children and your puppy so they all understand what are acceptable levels of interaction! Respect and trust is earned and they all have to earn the respect of the other!

We rarely consider the implications for the consequences of the behaviours that we establish in those first few hours of being together at home with our new puppy. Those first few hours at home with your new puppy are so important and applying the lessons you learn in this book will help you all get it right!

4 Top Tips on Arriving Home

1. Try to refrain from explaining your home to your puppy.
2. **Put a collar and lead on your puppy before you go into the house.**
3. Take your puppy outside on his collar and lead.
4. Do not reward excitement; calmly praise your puppy for being calm, thus establishing the correct associations from the word go.

It does sound strange to put a puppy in a collar and lead when you arrive at your house but it makes sense. Because your puppy will be keen to explore, he won't be bothered by the collar and lead and will walk nicely for you. You can then praise him for walking on a slack lead in a new environment as this is exactly how you want him to walk on a lead, isn't it?

By showing him around the house calmly, you are setting the right behavioural standards and you need to be praising him all the time he is calm and exploring nicely. Stop at regular intervals so he gets used to feeling the collar and lead tighten, when he stops and the lead slackens, praise him again as you are establishing good lead manners!

You won't need to keep the lead on all the time, but it starts off very good associations. Once you have explored the house and he has seen where he is allowed to be, then you can let him off but I would strongly recommend that you do further lead and collar sessions several times each day so you build good and relaxed associations for walking calmly on a slack lead.

Dogs and puppies are like us when it comes to learning, they learn through repetition and practice, they learn even quicker if you praise them when they are behaving how you want, would you enjoy your work if you were praised more?

It is these very behaviours, if correctly established, that the puppy will carry with him for the rest of his life.

4 Top Tips on Arriving Home

1. Try to refrain from explaining your home to your puppy.
2. Put a collar and lead on your puppy before you go into the house.
3. **Take your puppy outside on his collar and lead.**

4. Do not reward excitement; calmly praise your puppy for being calm, thus establishing the correct associations from the word go.

If your journey has been a long one, then an early consideration needs to be toilet time for your puppy. If you take your puppy straight into your house and allow them to explore with complete freedom, then you significantly increase the chances of the dog's first toilet being in the house and, again, this establishes a precedent that it is okay to toilet in the house. If your puppy's experience of first toilet is in the garden, you are also creating a positive experience and association from the outset. When your puppy toilets in the garden, give calm and relaxed verbal praise whilst he is going to the toilet, which helps your puppy create the correct association as you are providing reaction and interaction for it which reinforces the behaviour. By doing this on the lead, you also set the correct standard for walking on a lead outside. First impressions are so important!

You can also establish a toilet place because you have your puppy on the lead and can take him to the same place every time so he gets to associate that place as his toilet area. This is covered in more detail later in the book!

Your puppy needs to be calm outside to walk calmly so consider what expectations you are setting. If your puppy is encouraged to be excitable and play in the garden, he will expect to do the same when you take him for a walk, likewise, if you play with a ball in the garden, he will expect to be able to play with every ball he sees when he is out in the park so be aware what you set as acceptable standards of behaviour!

You have to remember that this is a baby and babies do not know how to behave, they merely follow examples so do not underestimate your responsibility and that of your family in shaping the correct behaviours from the outset for your puppy.

4 Top Tips on Arriving Home

1. Try to refrain from explaining your home to your puppy.
2. Put a collar and lead on your puppy before you go into the house.
3. Take your puppy outside on his collar and lead.
4. **Do not reward excitement; calmly praise your puppy for being calm, thus establishing the correct associations from the word go.**

The interaction that you give your puppy, especially verbal and physical interaction is your puppy is only clue about how you want him to behave. The problem for us with that is the new puppy is the centre of attention and he gets attention for everything he does from everybody.

Just consider that for a moment, the puppy gets attention for everything he does from everybody.

This means, in real life terms, you are teaching your puppy that you will always be there, you will always give attention for everything and always. Now ask yourself, is that a realistic expectation to set? Are you able to fulfill this expectation for the rest of your dogs life?

If the answer is yes, then you will never be able to leave your dog on his own, if your answer is no then you are setting yourself up to fail because you also will never be able to leave your dog on his own.

Now you may be asking why?

If you condition your puppy to expect all of your attention all the time, how is your puppy supposed to behave when you do leave him on his own? Because you are going to have to, aren't you?

It is impossible to be with the your dog all the time, isn't it?

So you can see the importance of establishing the behaviours you want and how you do this by your own behaviour and how you interact with your puppy. It is essential, if you want a happy and positive relationship for the whole life of your dog that your foundations are strong.

This can only be achieved by clear communication from the outset. Now this is probably making sense to you but also leaving you with a question. You probably understand the need to be calm and to reward your puppy with your attention for being calm so that becomes accepted normal behaviour but what about playing with him? Read on and you will find out!

Speaking of high levels of attention leads me nicely into ….

SEPARATION ANXIETY

The root cause of separation anxiety is the setting of unsustainable levels of attention.

Let me expand on that further. If your puppy is taught to expect your attention for being excited, active and stressed, usually through extended periods of play the whole time he is awake, as well as lots of cuddles and fuss, when you remove your attention your puppy will become more stressed because he is not getting the attention he has come to expect so he escalates his stress and begins to behave badly because he expects to get attention for being stressed and confused and this is when puppies become destructive when left alone. It's also why they bark, howl or whine for the attention you have shown them to be normal.

You greeting your puppy in an excited manner when you arrive home and by saying goodbye to him or worse, giving him a treat when you leave, further establish this expectation. This is then exacerbated further when, upon your return you find puppy has been destructive or has been messy because you will tell the puppy off. This merely teaches your puppy to be stressed when you leave and that you will immediately make them stressed upon your return, thus conditioning your puppy to associate stress with you. Not exactly the best start in life is it?

So, if orally telling my puppy off for wrong doing rewards that behaviour, then how can you stop your puppy misbehaving?

This is often the stumbling block for dog and puppy owners alike and it can be quite difficult to strike the balance, particularly with our need as humans to talk, and oh boy, do we feel the need to talk! Please read on and you will understand how to achieve this!

Toilet Training

No guide to puppies would be complete without a guide to toilet training so here is a different take

Your new puppy does not know what you want him to do, dogs don't know what you want them to do. They are very good at reading us and getting to know our behavioural patterns but they are not telepathic, neither do they do things to annoy or frustrate us. We have to help them and show them what we want and then use our voices to let them know they have done well and teaching your new puppy where to toilet is no exception. You have to remember that your puppy is a baby with little control of his bodily functions and he has always gone to the toilet in the area he lived with his mum. He has absolutely no idea that you want him to toilet outside; he just sees your home as a bigger area than the one he is used to where his mum cleans him after he has gone to the toilet.

Plus, he already has a routine for his toilet but no one has bothered to take any notice let alone explain it to you so you at least have some idea of the frequency and times of his routine. This is because his breeders probably spent their time fussing and playing with them rather than observing them and learning his habits and timings. Puppies tend to toilet shortly after they wake up, shortly after they have eaten and about half way through playtime with their siblings.

They learn these timings from their mother because in the first three weeks, she licks them to stimulate their bodily functions and so sets the timings they follow. Now you will be pleased to hear that your new puppy does not need you to lick anything but they do need you to be observant and learn their patterns because you can then time your intervention and removal to your chosen toilet place properly so you can quickly teach your dog house manners. I work with many owners whose dogs are still not house trained at six months or even older. Take the time to get it right from the start and you will reap the benefits.

Puppies are already creatures of habit and they do give indicators that they are ready to toilet, the signs, however, are easily missed! As always with our dogs, you will learn the most simply by sitting and watching because you will then get to know your new puppy properly and in the right way, calm and relaxed!

4 Top Tips on Toilet Training

1. **Be patient**
2. Put a collar and lead on your puppy before you go outside the house.
3. Keep your puppy calm
4. Do not punish your puppy if a mistake happens

Patience is the key. Your puppy is a baby and whilst he will learn quickly, it is your job now to make sure you give the best possible help. By getting to know your puppy through calm and relaxed observation, you will quickly realise there are certain times when he will want to toilet, after eating and upon waking up after a sleep. Whilst this is true, don't rush him outside as soon as he has eaten or wakes up, take your time.

Where is his toilet?

This is a key question. Is the whole garden his toilet or would you like him to use just one area? If he can use the whole garden then let him toilet anywhere. If you want him to use one area, put his lead on and take him to the area you want him to use. Be patient, when he toilets, calmly praise with your voice so he associates verbal reward with relieving himself in your chosen area. Patience is the key, as he may not toilet immediately. Letting him sniff the ground will also help him stimulate bodily functions!

He will only be a baby for a short time so it is time well spent teaching toilet behaviours. I work with many dogs that are still not house trained at a year old, because the time was not taken to teach the puppy properly in the first place.

You are setting examples of behaviour. If your puppy gets played with outside, you will make house training more difficult because your puppy will associate being outside with rushing round and being excited and active. Puppies and dogs all learn better when they are calm and relaxed.

4 Top Tips on Toilet Training

1. Be patient
2. **Put a collar and lead on your puppy before you go outside the house.**
3. Keep your puppy calm
4. Do not punish your puppy if a mistake happens

This is usually the first time your new puppy goes outside the house with you so it gives you an opportunity to teach the behaviours you want outside the house. If your puppy is granted complete freedom in your garden, then he will expect complete freedom when on a walk, taking the puppy to a park usually reinforces this and giving him complete freedom when he is old enough and then we wonder why we have no recall!!

If you take your puppy into the garden on a collar and lead, you can ensure you establish the toilet area and you can ensure your puppy is calm on a lead with you when outside. This will prove invaluable when you do for a walk because your puppy will already have experience of walking with you calmly on a lead.

When your puppy has finished his toilet, have a calm walk around the garden, let him go to the end of the lead and then call him back to you. When he comes to you, praise with calm and slow stroking. After all, you want your puppy to like being with you don't you?

If you praise vigorously and loudly, your puppy will quickly go away from you, which is not the situation you want, is it? You want your puppy to want to be with you, so make being with you nice and relaxed.

See how much you can achieve in these first few days and weeks just by having the lead on? The basics are best learned when you have your puppies undivided attention so you can set the foundation for the weeks and months ahead!

4 Top Tips on Toilet Training

1. Be patient
2. Put a collar and lead on your puppy before you go outside the house.
3. **Keep your puppy calm**
4. Do not punish your puppy if a mistake happens

There is a very good reason for keeping your puppy calm and that is mistake prevention. Mistakes can be prevented if sufficient warning is given and the warnings are recognised and acted upon. If your puppy is calm, there will be sufficient time for you to recognise the signs that he wants to toilet and act upon them by getting your puppy outside to his toilet area in good time. This makes the whole experience calm and pleasant, one your puppy will be keen to repeat because we all like to repeat pleasant experiences, don't we?

So, if your puppy is not calm, and the best example of this is a puppy that is played with a lot, he will not have the time to show you the warnings because they won't have the time to recognise them themselves because they are too active and too busy. All of a sudden, the feeling of desperation is upon them and they have to let go, wherever they are and whatever they are doing.

So you see, if your new puppy makes a mistake, it is really your fault, not theirs because you have not given them the time they need to recognise the signs they need to toilet. Time and patience are the key factors in all teaching, even more so with your new puppy so don't rush and put yourself and your new puppy under too much pressure, it will affect your budding relationship.

We should give our puppies every chance to succeed, to get it right so we can build a mutual relationship based on trust and respect so make the effort to get it right, especially with toileting because it can be the cause of a great deal of frustration and confusion!

4 Top Tips on Toilet Training

1. Be patient
2. Put a collar and lead on your puppy before you go outside the house.

3. Keep your puppy calm

4. **Do not punish your puppy if a mistake happens**

As I alluded to in the previous section, if your puppy has made a mistake and toileted in the house, then it is because you have failed to spot the signs in time to take your puppy outside. Puppies do not toilet inside to annoy you so please do not rub their noses in it, you are only teaching your puppy to mistrust you, especially as they don't know any different yet. Your puppy has performed an essential bodily function merely in the wrong place. If you were looking after a human baby and they messed whilst you were changing their nappy, would you rub their faces in the mess? I certainly hope not, it would only upset them and teach them you are behaving in a very strange way, the same applies to your puppy. They are trying their best to learn your rules and learning how to behave for you so please make that experience as relaxed and positive because they will learn quicker that way.

Your puppy is relying on you for direction, leadership, love and boundaries and needs you to be calm and relaxed.

Shouting at your puppy only teaches fear and mistrust because they don't understand why you are behaving that way, hitting your puppy makes your puppy fear you and your hands because that behaviour is very confusing and painful. Using loud noises can easily make a confident puppy a nervous wreck so don't use fear, force or stress with your puppy. You can see how our own instinctive reactions, and those we have been told to do by other dog owners can be damaging to your puppy because they do not consider the puppies perspective.

Teach your puppy to expect your attention for being calm and relaxed and he will transfer this belief to all of his behaviours.

When you achieve what you want and need with toilet training, you will have a puppy that you can take into other people's houses and have the confidence that he will toilet as you have taught him. This does depend on the other people being calm with your puppy. Other people can undo all of your training at this stage so make sure your friends and family respect your wishes and rules. When they do, your puppy will be able to make extraordinary progress and make you justifiably proud!

I hope you found this section useful and I also hope it has helped you appreciate a little more just how important your behaviour is in the first two days can be. Good luck with your new puppy!

How to Play With Your Puppy

An over excited puppy will be a problem and will give you problems that will need sorting out yet are entirely of your own creation.

This is a very difficult part of raising a puppy, particularly if you have young children in the house as they will want to play with the children. When a puppy is played with too much as a puppy, by both children and adults this causes a great deal of frustration, which leads to problem behaviours in the adult dog and these include:

1. High frustration that can lead to aggression
2. Biting
3. Chasing
4. Barking
5. Lunging when on the lead
6. Stealing items of clothing etc

7. Destructive behaviour
8. A complete lack of respect

The adult dog can and will apply these behaviours to adults and children. These are just a few examples of unwanted adult behaviours that can be traced back to puppyhood and behaviours that were learned through excessive play which creates a belief of excitement around children and the other members of the family. I deal with many dogs that become boisterous and nippy around children, and these behaviours can also be transferred to adults as they try to intervene.

Rules of play are very important and the types of play also play a major part in teaching your puppy how to behave for you.

Play is by definition competitive and teaching your dog it is allowed, even encouraged to compete with you can lead to problems later in life. Now this does not apply to all dogs, as dogs are individual as we are but you need to be aware of the potential consequences for teaching your dog it can compete with you.

You are going to need your dog to be under control and for your dog to trust and respect you and playing, particularly playing with toys or in games where there has to be a winner can condition your dog into unwanted behaviours. Your relationship with your dog should be based on mutual trust and respect rather than a need to be constantly trying to out do each other. You will tire of the competition long before your dog will!!

So, if you still insist on playing with your dog, I will put down some guidelines for you to follow. Before I do, you will notice I said, "If you still insist on playing with your dog."

My choice of words is deliberate because I do not advocate playing with your dog; I believe your dog should associate interaction with you with calm and relaxed behaviour.

You may consider this boring, you may think it is essential to play with your puppy and this belief suggests you are playing with your dog for your own benefit without regard for the needs of your puppy. I see too many puppies and dogs who, when a man walks into the house get very excited and fetch toys just because their owner has played with them. They transfer these behaviours to every individual who fits the bill and not everyone wants to play with your dog!

We have to understand the consequences of what we teach our dogs to do because they stretch far outside the limits we operate in!

So, for those who still insist in playtime with their dogs I encourage you to follow these guidelines.

First, observe your puppy when he is playing by himself. Observe his levels of excitement, the duration of his play and when he chooses to stop. He is showing you how he wants to play, he is showing you what he can cope with and if we choose to override this, we are doing our puppy the greatest disservice because we are ignoring his needs.

Second, you decide when playtime starts. Do not start playtime on your puppies terms so if your puppy brings you a toy, the game does not start otherwise your puppy is learning to control your attention with toys.

Third, you only play with your puppy with a toy that you keep just for play. Do not play with your puppies toys or he will bring you these as you have given them power of attention.

Fourth, the game only starts when your dog is calm, this is why you do not respond to the dogs demands for a game as the dog is already wound up. This would also mean you are rewarding excitement!

Fifth, limit the level at which you play, remember watching your puppy playing by himself and how he was still calm when playing. If your puppy starts to growl or put his teeth on you, even gently, you have gone too far and the game should stop and they toy gets put away and you must then let your puppy calm down.

Sixth, you must clam the dog down and then calmly stroke the calm dog so you leave the dog as you found it, calm and relaxed. If you leave the dog in an excited state, he will go and bring his own toys and try to make you continue the game.

Playing with your dog beyond his ability to cope can build stress and frustration in your dog. These are not the feelings you want your dog have for you and this is why I urge caution when you consider playing with your dog because the human condition is not predisposed toward calm and controlled play. We nearly always over excite our puppy and this is why games can often get out of hand. How many times have I heard an owner excuse the bite he has just received from his puppy as "he was only playing" as the blood oozes down his hand!

Dog's interpretation of play is very different to ours, dog use play as youngsters to practice hunting skills and to test their strength and confidence up to about six months old. When these skills are learned, they stop playing! We play for entertainment and fun so the two interpretations are completely different and this is why dogs find it difficult to understand what we are doing and how they are supposed to respond. Especially when we continue to play with them for their whole lives and at ever increasing levels.

Play also unleashes the competitive streak in both puppy and human, especially when men play with puppies because men tend to push escalation to the point where there must be a winner. This is the most dangerous game you can play because you might be the winner when your puppy is young and small, however when your dog is fully-grown and mature the outcome may well be very different and then you are in serious trouble. Once the dog is the winner and he believes he can win, he is very difficult to get back under control as he has lost all respect for you because you forced the contest and you forced him to win!

Your puppy needs you to look after him not force him to compete with you. People who play with their puppies do so for their own needs, not those of their dog and their relationship is out of balance because of that. We should be working with our dogs, not teaching them to compete with us!

Beware what you allow your dog to do; you will reap what you sow!

Crate Training

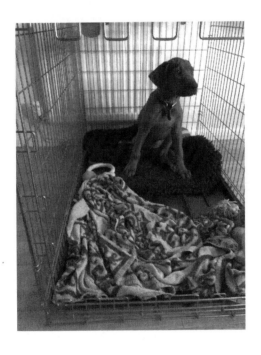

One of the most important and least considered parts of getting a new puppy is the first night. Everyone is so excited to get the new puppy home and play with him that preparing him for his first night is largely forgotten until it is bedtime. But you have taken him away from everything he knows and feels safe with and put him a noisy and busy environment where he is the centre of attention. It is really unfair to not only expect your new puppy to cope with his new house, family and a great deal of attention, we then expect him to also cope when all those people suddenly disappear. He doesn't know you have all just gone to bed and will come back tomorrow; he is suddenly alone for the first time in his life. Is it any wonder he cries and whimpers? He is scared, alone and frightened.

Just as you thought you had done all the preparation you needed, I spring this on you. As if you haven't got enough to do on the first day your puppy comes home, we have to also try to build in preparing him for his first night.

But it needn't be as daunting as it sounds if it is thought through properly and prepared properly so this chapter is all about how you can properly prepare your new puppy for his first night during his first day with you.

But it needs careful planning which is why I have included this chapter fairly close to the start of the book so preparation for nighttime is something you are thinking about as soon as possible.

One of the most important considerations is where is puppy going to sleep? You may have read up on this and there will be many different views but mine is a simple one and a practical one. Your puppy needs to spend the night in a place close to the back door because the first few weeks are going to be all about toilet training aren't they? If your puppy is close to the back door, it is easier to get him outside to go to the toilet isn't it? If he is upstairs or in a room further away from the back door, his chances of making a mistake are higher. Another advantage of having him near the back door is nighttime toilet. Many people are finding that coming down in the night to let their new puppy out for the toilet is speeding up the toilet training process but I advise a word of caution. If you do this, please make sure you don't give your puppy any attention. Just take him out, let him toilet and then put him back to bed. If you give him attention, he may well start to make a noise at 2am to get you to come down and talk to him! I know that's a tough ask, but a very important one!

But I have strayed slightly off point. Where is your new puppy going to spend his first night? It doesn't really matter where, what is really going to matter is being on his own for the very first time and how he deals with it.

You can see why this is a difficult thing to plan into your new puppy's first day because the last thing he is going to be on his first day is on his own. Why? Because he will be completely inundated with attention if people have their way so you need to be in control of the whole situation, even more challenging if you have young children in the house!

So, where is puppy going to sleep and how will you prepare him for his first night?

For the first time in his life, he is going to experience enforced isolation. Now that may sound harsh but that's exactly what your puppy's first night will be and this needs to be planned. So now you have decided which room your new puppy will spend their first night in, I hope it is the room next to the back door that is probably the kitchen. This is a good idea because the kitchen probably has a hard floor that is easy to clean. Is your puppy going to be given a lovely new bed to sleep in or are you going to introduce a crate for him? These are also big decisions to make and are important. You will need to consider your own wishes here too. A puppy with just a bed to sleep in is more likely to explore during the night and he may encounter things he doesn't understand. When exploring, a puppy's first instinct is to put his mouth on the new object he has discovered, if it requires further understanding, he may well decide to chew. If you are in bed, how can you help and guide him into a behaviour you want? You can't and it is just as impossible to be up all night with him but we need to make sure he is safe so the best solution is a crate. You see, even if you have another dog, your new puppy will still explore and get into mischief. Plus it is entirely unfair to leave your established dog at the mercy of a new puppy for a whole night so a crate is the best solution for all of you.

You can go to bed knowing your puppy is safe and can't bother your other dog, if you have one. You can go to bed knowing your new puppy feels secure can't you? Wait a minute, knowing your puppy is safe is one thing but is he going to feel secure?

Now that is a whole different consideration because your new puppy is not going to feel secure. He has left his mum and siblings, they all used to snuggle up together at night when they were together and that is how your puppy felt secure. So we have a challenge don't we? His first night is going to be cold, quiet and lonely. Now you can see why you new puppy is going to be confused during his first night and how the first day has to be done properly.

So here is the plan for getting a good first night and for this to become a consistent pattern so the majority of nights are good ones. You might not agree with or feel comfortable with this plan as it will go against many of the things you think you should do with a new puppy on his first day but you will be very glad you did when you get consistently quiet nights.

This is the method I use when I introduce a new dog or puppy into my house so it based on sound practice and it does work.

I won't break it down into bullet points because it isn't really a step by step approach, it isn't a list, it's more of a way of doing things that matter..

My first point is a question. Did you get a blanket from the breeder that smells of his mum and siblings? Did you put the blanket into a plastic bag so your smell does not reduce that of his mum and siblings? Have you got a heat lamp organised or placed his crate by a radiator if you have your heating on?

So your new puppy feels less stressed upon arrival in his new home, we need to help him make the transition into his crate and to make sure his first experience of his crate is a pleasant, positive and relaxing one His crate is going to remind him of feeling warm and secure, hence the blanket with smells of home on. He doesn't know your smell yet so why would he find comfort in it yet? He can only get to know your smell if he spends the whole day on your knee and is just not sustainable is it as he can't spend all night on you knee can he?

So making sure you have followed the advice I gave in the getting him home chapters in the first part of this book, you bring him into the house on his lead and you put the blanket from his breeder into his crate taking care not to handle it yourself so the smells of home remain strong. The heat lamp should already be on or the heating is on so his crate is nice and warm. Put him on the floor in front of the open crate, let him sniff and wander in. This is making a good association with the crate from the outset. If he settles down in the crate, close and lock the door and walk away. Wait a minute, come back, open the crate door and pick up his lead. Don't give eye contact or talk at this point, just see what he wants to do. If he comes out, then continue to walk him on his lead around your home. After 15 minutes, walk him back to the crate and stop at the open door. If he walks in and settles, close the door, walk away for a couple of minutes and open the door again. Pick up the lead and see what he wants to do.

If he settles into a sleep, close the door and walk away and get on with something else. He clearly feels secure in his crate and likes being in there. That is a good association established. As soon as he starts to wake up, go to the crate, open the door, pick up his lead and take him outside for the toilet. When he goes, calmly praise him. Walk him back into the house and continue to walk him around on the lead. After half an hour, take him back to his crate and let him walk in. Close the door and go away for five minutes.

Let him hear and get used to the sounds of your house and the people that live in it. After five minutes come back and get him and continue to walk him around the house on the lead.

You see you are establishing a pattern that your new puppy understands. The crate is a nice place to be, he does get shut in and you do come and get him and this happens on a regular basis. So when bedtime comes, he already has good and positive experience of being in his crate on his own.

There is still something else we can do to help him be relaxed in his crate at night. We have provided smells he is familiar with and his crate his warm but what else has he been used to? Breathing, he is used to the sounds of his mum and siblings breathing. If you have planned above and beyond what people usually do, you may have asked the breeder for a recording of him and his siblings sleeping so you can play it during those first few nights so he can feel lovely and secure. If you didn't think that far ahead, get your hands on a meditation or relaxation cd that has sounds of deep breathing as you can play this during his first few nights as he won't feel so alone. Leaving a radio or TV on does not help or soothe, it is just a background noise. Sleeping in the same room will help but your puppy can become dependent on that plus you are then far more inclined to give your puppy attention rather than just being company that is why a cd is the much better option.

This is all well and good and it works beautifully but it depends on one major factor and that is you and your family is calm and relaxed with your new puppy. If you excite and wind up your puppy, you will make it very difficult for your puppy to learn anything except being excited gets a lot of attention and believe me, that is the cause of the vast majority of dog behaviour problems. If you keep you and your family calm, your puppy will be calm and will learn what you want him to learn. If you are excitable and react with your voice, your puppy will learn exactly what you don't want him to learn. The principles in this book apply to the whole life of your dog. If you apply them for the whole life of your dog, you will learn so much and enjoy so much more of the time you spend together.

How to Deal with biting

4 Top Tips on Dealing With Biting:

1. **Why puppies bite**
2. How to deal with a bite
3. Distraction
4. Do not punish your puppy for biting

All puppies bite things they encounter, it is a sensory requirement whilst they learn about the world around them. Human babies explore the world by putting things they touch with their hands into their mouths and puppies are only a little different. Because they have no hands, they put the world in their mouth to learn about taste, texture, hardness, softness, noise and movement. Puppies have natural instincts that are stimulated by movement and noise so if something is noisy and moving, the puppy is going to bite it. If the thing the puppy bites then moves more and makes more noise, then your puppy will become more and more excited. He won't know why he is getting stimulated; he knows he can't help it at his tender age. At this tender age, your puppy will not know what he can or can't bite. As he explores his new world, he will explore with his mouth and he will make mistakes. He won't know he is making mistakes but, as with all dog behaviour, it is how we react to his use of his mouth and associated behaviour that persuades him to stop or keep mouthing or chewing. Our reaction to his behaviour determines the success or failure of that behaviour. If behaviour generates no attention or reaction, then that behaviour will quickly loose your puppy's interest. However, if behaviour generates attention then that behaviour has a value and is worth repeating.

Of all your puppies behaviours, biting is the one that is most likely to generate a reaction and attention. This means it can be a very easy behaviour to create and reinforce from a very early age so being aware of your behaviour is very important indeed!

Lets go back to noise and movement. What is the part of you that your puppy quickly associates with movement and noise? Your hands of course! Your hands stroke your puppy and stimulate your puppy through play and you make a noise when doing so. You are then fulfilling the two main stimuli for biting, noise and movement! Then you complain your puppy has bitten you yet it was your lack of understanding that provoked the bite!

As with all learning, patience is the key and the more frustrated you get, the more frustrated and confused your puppy will get so patience is the key. Your puppy will trust you more quickly if his mistakes don't frustrate you. Remember, your voice means reward to your puppy so don't tell him off of he makes a mistake, stay calm and relaxed.

4 Top Tips on Dealing With Biting:

1. Why puppies bite
2. **How to deal with a bite**
3. Distraction
4. Do not punish your puppy for biting

With all unwanted behaviours, prevention is better than cure, which is great if you had all the information you needed before you got a puppy. It is also true of human nature that we only tend to try and fix a problem when it has become a major one, rather than seeing the problem at the start and then dealing with is when it is much more easily resolved.

There are many different ways to deal with a bite from a puppy, or your puppy putting teeth on to you. There is a difference between your puppy biting and your puppy putting teeth on to you but either way he needs to learn this is not an acceptable behaviour.

As you get to know your puppy and your puppy gets to know you, your interaction will discover the threshold your puppy has to deal with stimulation. If you play with him, fuss him quickly, you will provoke a bite or he will put teeth on to you due to the over stimulation. It's all part of you're learning process and you will have read, during your research of the oracle that is the internet a myriad of different ways to deal with a puppy bite from squealing to making the puppy bite himself or worse, biting your puppy yourself!!

All of these are far from ideal, they will not resolve the issue and they won't generate trust and clear communication between you and your puppy. Remember, your puppy has bitten or put teeth on you because of overstimulation so anything that provides more stimulation can only make things worse. Your reaction to your puppy biting you has to be calm and relaxed, even if he is hurting you! Puppy teeth are very sharp and will hurt and I do appreciate it is difficult to remain calm but remember he is not biting you because he doesn't like you he is exploring behaviours.

If he bites your hand, relax the hand he has hold of and move it away from him. Avoid eye contact, don't speak to him and stand up. This teaches him that putting teeth on you makes you go away. This shows him his decision to put teeth on you has made the source of his attention go away, it becomes a counter productive behaviour.

Sit down again and go to stroke your puppy. If he puts teeth on again, stand up again, count to 10 and sit down. Repeat this until you can stroke him calmly and he remains calm. This way, you are showing him that your hands don't wind him up; instead they are a source of calm and relaxing attention. By doing this, the calmer he stays, the more attention he gets and you are rewarding the correct behaviour in the correct way.

If, however, he does bite you and you can't remove your hand, this approach will work but only if you do it slowly and calmly. Avoid eye contact and speaking to him, relax the hand in his mouth and with your other hand, take hold of his collar and gently hold him still without having a tight grip on the collar. He will quickly realise that nothing is happening and he will open his mouth, when he does calmly remove your hand and then calmly stroke and praise. You won't feel like praising him and you may feel like you are praising him for biting you. You are not because you are praising him for what he is doing, not what he has done! Try to avoid making the same mistake again by keeping you both calmer in the future.

The key part of the above is that your puppy is wearing a collar. If he is not then you are far more limited to how you can deal with a bite because grabbing his fur or skin will only add to his stimulation and make the situation more stressful and confusing for him. Stimulation and agitation can have an adverse affect on a puppy and the last thing you want your new puppy to learn is adverse behaviours, especially if it involves biting. These behaviours are much easier to prevent in a puppy than they are to cure in an adult so to start as you mean to go on make sure your puppy is wearing a collar!

4 Top Tips on Dealing With Biting:

1. Why puppies bite
2. How to deal with a bite
3. **Distraction**
4. Do not punish your puppy for biting

Distraction and interruption can be a very useful tactic in teaching your puppy how you want him to behave when he is exploring and finding out about his new home. Because your puppy interprets hearing your voice and his name as a reward for his behaviour, it is impossible to tell a puppy to stop doing something but it does work if you give him an alternative and I am not talking about treats or food! If you use food or treats to distract your puppy from what he is doing, your puppy probably will come to you. But he will also quickly learn to repeat the behaviour in order to get a treat; yes he is that clever! Your puppy will also be excited for his treat so you are still rewarding excitement, not relaxation. You want your puppy to be calm so why use a reward that prevents that happening? It just does not make sense to me when you are trying to teach your puppy to be calm!

Once you have shown your puppy the house on the lead and how you want him to behave, you are going to have to let him explore on his own but under your supervision so you are going to have to take the lead off!

When, and he will, tries to chew something you don't want him to chew, a very useful tip is to click your fingers and make a squeak by breathing in through pursed lips. The combination of these sounds will get his attention on to you and he will probably come back to you. If he does, you can calmly praise him for you have just achieved your first recall!! If he doesn't come to you, make the squeak last longer. He will find this difficult to ignore and he is then more likely to respond and come to you. When he does, he needs lots of nice calm praise to reward such a great decision!

This also sets a very important precedent in your puppy's mind that he has to come to you to get any attention. To do this he has to come away from the object he was interested in which is the perfect demonstration of what you want. Teaching your puppy he has to come away from an object of interest to you for attention is the best thing your puppy will ever do. It is the perfect recall and needs to practised as often as possible and in as many different situations as possible. This is a true win-win situation that establishes clear communication and understanding with a lovely reward for coming to you, excellent!

By taking this approach, you are able to remain calmer and the more relaxed you are, the quicker your puppy will learn to trust you and the greater the bond. Earning trust is the most essential part of your relationship so getting off to the right start is essential and so very rewarding.

This way your voice is used at the right time to only reward and praise so your voice and the use of your puppies name becomes very important to your puppy. When your puppy hears your voice and his name all the time, especially for telling him off, he learns to ignore it and it becomes background noise so learn to use your voice when it matters most, to reward good behaviour and your dog will be very attentive when you do speak.

4 Top Tips on Dealing With Biting:

1. Why puppies bite
2. How to deal with a bite
3. Distraction
4. **Do not punish your puppy for biting**

Punishing your dog just does not work at any age. Trying to punish a puppy is just as futile because your puppy does not understand what you are doing because they do not think like we do. They do not understand right or wrong or good or bad. They do what they think they should do and gauge our reaction. It is our reactions that give a behaviour value or render behaviour pointless.

Biting can be a perfectly natural activity for your puppy and your puppy needs to be guided into understanding that not biting is your preferred behaviour. Your puppy cannot and will not learn if you make him fearful, confused and stressed. After all, you are supposed to be earning your puppies trust and shaping good behaviour, what kind of example are you setting if you turn into a screaming monster whose noise and activity terrify your puppy? Would trust a guide or teacher if they behaved like that?

You must remember that you are working with a baby and this baby is not a human being. He is a baby that is trying his very best to fit in to a very strange and new world. In his struggle to make sense of it, he tries many different behaviours to see what gets your attention, this is his way of learning so take a step back and try to appreciate life from his perspective.

Your puppy does not know how to behave, he does not know what you want, he doesn't know you really so you are both learning new skills and learning about each other. It's impossible to explain to your puppy what you want and expect of him. He will never speak or understand your language and you will never speak or fully understand his.

Accept that as fact and learn to still your voice until your puppy is behaving well enough to deserve your voice and attention.

Take the pressure off by giving yourself and your puppy the time and opportunity to make mistakes so you can both learn in a calm and relaxed environment. Take time to observe and learn each other's ways. Spend these precious first few days and weeks doing this because you will reap the benefit for the rest of the time you have together.

Relationships between people always get off to uncertain starts and only improve as you get to know and trust each other and the best relationships are based on mutual trust and respect. Your relationship with your new puppy is built in exactly the same way. You have a great responsibility for your new puppy as their life is literally in your hands so please do your very best to get it right, your puppy will thank you for it!

I want to finish with two points.

Firstly I want you to believe and accept that you are not compatible with every dog and every dog is not compatible with you. The amount of dogs in rescue centres proves this. But also remember this, our behaviours can change a perfectly compatible dog into one we cannot live with. This is the easiest part for you to get wrong. When you get it wrong and your dog has gone to the rescue centre, it is then someone else's job to undo your work to make your dog compatible again. If your dog is too much for the rescue centre, your dog will die. It takes very special skills to work with the worst dogs. Take the time and the right approach to ensure your dog is compatible with you.

Secondly, I want to introduce to you the medal table concept for attention to help you understand what your different levels of attention mean to your puppy or dog.

As with all medal tables there are three levels of award, bronze, silver and gold and these grade attention in importance in the same way when real medals are awarded to athletes.

So, isn't the attention medal table, what level of your attention qualifies as bronze?

Stroking or other fuss from your hands qualifies as the bronze standard of attention.

What level of your attention qualifies as the silver standard of attention?

Speaking and talking with the use of your puppy's name qualifies as the silver standard of attention.

Which leads us to the top level of the winners podium. What level of your attention qualifies as the gold standard of attention?

Your eye contact is the absolute holy grail of attention, the best your dog can get and the level of your attention your puppy desires the most. Why is eye contact so desirable for your puppy or dog?

It is the ultimate in attention because your eye contact means your puppy has your undivided attention, you are then his to manipulate as he sees fit in order to get the gold standard of attention.

Now stop and ask your self how often do you give your dog a gold medal? Now ask your self which of his behaviours get your gold medal? If he gets your gold medal for being calm and relaxed then you can give yourself a gold medal because you are doing it right!

In reality, you are giving him your gold standard of attention for the behaviours you don't want instead of rewarding his best behaviour with gold. But it is probably worse than that because you are probably giving him a silver medal at the same time as the gold! This just doubly reinforces his unwanted behaviour rather than doubly reinforcing his best behaviour. I could write a whole other book on how dogs learn patterns of behaviour from our verbal and eye contact, it is an amazing field of understanding when you begin to explore it from your puppy's perspective!

CONCLUSION

It's All About You!

Science has, over the past ten years made huge strides in understanding how dogs learn, what they are capable of and how they have learned to live with us and the dog has emerged as a far more complex animal than previously thought. Research has, to my knowledge, only scratched the surface of the dog/human relationship and I don't think there are any studies about how our reactions shape our dogs behaviour in the real world outside of the training or research environment.

This is where there is a huge gap in knowledge and this gap is the cause of the very serious problems that result in the serious injury or the death of a person. The media report the very worst of these problems but there are many more dogs out there that are a ticking bomb. These instances are usually preventable and are usually the result of learned behaviours that can be traced back to the dog's early life.

So, my dear reader, in conclusion, its all about you! You may not have even considered just how involved you are in your puppies development, after all, dogs just fit in, don't they?

Nothing could be further from the truth. If you see a well behaved dog, it is not an accident nor is the owner just lucky, it is the result of dedication and consistency that has brought out the best behaviour in the dog, which in turn brings out the best behaviour in the owner and so the positive spirals.

You only get out what you put in and that applies to all relationships, even more so with our dogs because of the language barrier. Dogs have a far greater understanding of our behaviour than we have of theirs. Their attention to detail is vastly superior to ours because their communication is non-verbal and very subtle which makes it very easy to miss. Our puppies and dogs have to pay attention to get our attention yet we give our attention away for at best nothing or, at worst the very behaviours we do not want.

It is because we miss the non-verbal and the subtle that our dogs have learned to bark. They have learned to bark because shouting at us is sometimes the only way they can get our attention. It is sad that an animal you class as your best friend is forced to shout at you just to feel involved.

Obedience training is fine for what it is, behaviour advice that uses clicker or food is missing the point, one off behaviour visits or assessments do not work because human nature and my experience of training dog owners proves you will revert to type without the opportunity to practice and learn. Any training or behaviour advice that involves force, punishment, harsh corrections or the use of fear or pain is prehistoric and should be avoided at all costs. Any trainer or behaviourist who uses choke chains, pinch (prong) collars or electric collars is using tools that inflict pain on your dog and these people should be reported to the police and the RSPCA. Any trainer that advocates the yanking and strong pulling of your dog is using out of date dominance theories. None of these will ever improve your dogs behaviour nor will they improve the relationship you have with your dog.

Your puppy and your dog need you to understand them better, they need you to take the time to get to know then properly in a calm and relaxed environment. They would love it of you took the time to spot their subtle signals and then learned how to answer.

I love my dogs, I want my dogs to be happy and have the best life I can give them. To me that mean I can take my dogs anywhere and they are well behaved so I am proud to be seen with them. They trust me to be calm and relaxed whatever situation we come across because that means they can stay calm and relaxed. Through this understanding, we have developed a great deal of trust and mutual respect so we love spending time together.

The relationship you envisage with your dog is achievable but like all relationships, it takes time, patience and practice. If you are prepared to put the work and effort in, your dog will love you as much as you love him and will be a very well behaved part of your life.

If you are not prepared to put the time, patience and practice in then please do not get a dog because dogs deserve more than you, they deserve better than you so please wait until you can commit the necessary resources and time to ensure success.

When you pay closer attention to your dog, you will start to notice the details, you will start to notice the subtle changes in their behaviour which is our dogs simply giving us choices about which behaviour to reward. These are so easily missed yet when recognised and a timely answer is given, you can start to have a real conversation with your dog that you both understand and that is a thing of real beauty and an immense feeling.

Open you eyes to your dog start to observe and learn and you will be surprised, very surprised!

Thank you for reading my approach to puppy behaviour, I wish you a happy and relaxed life with your dog!

ABOUT THE AUTHOR

Steven Havers

Steven Havers has been working with dogs for 20 years, for the past eight years full time. He is a professional dog behaviourist, to give him a title you will recognise but the reality is very different because Steven does not train dogs how to behave. Steven trains the dog's owners how to behave and their dogs follow the lead.

Because of his time working with dogs, Steven has used most of the historic techniques but has realised these techniques don't add to the relationship with his dogs and it was this realisation that helped him develop his proven method of retraining the owner to realise and understand how they should behave.

Steven has competed with his dogs in the disciplines of tracking, obedience and protection so he understands first hand the difference between training and behaviour which is why he will tell you "you can't have a well trained dog until you have a well behaved dog"

It is a very simple idea yet was very difficult to arrive at and Steven arrived at this conclusion when he realised that dogs do not learn to misbehave because they are stroked, fussed or treated at the wrong time, they learn to misbehave because they get spoken to, often shouted at for the wrong behaviour so the failing must be with the owners.

When he applied this theory to his own dogs, then to other peoples dogs, he was amazed at how well the dogs understood the different communication and how quickly they were willing to change.

So, in Stevens training sessions, you will not see food or treats, no toys or balls, any choke chains or adverse methods. You will simply see him teaching owners how to use a lead properly, how to properly socialise your dog and how your praise will overcome even the worst behaviour.

The idea is different; the application can be difficult for some people yet the results are amazing.

Through understanding comes knowledge and Steven understands how human behaviour shapes that of our dogs at levels you can only begin to imagine. His attention to detail has to be seen to believed because he sees things in your dog that you never will yet once you see them they are obvious.

You can learn more about Steven on his website:
www.haversdogbehaviour.co.uk

23738351R00067

Printed in Great Britain
by Amazon